Well of Sparrow Song

Poems by Joel Matthews

Kansas City Spartan Press Missouri

Spartan Press
Kansas City, Missouri
spartanpresskc.com

Copyright (c) Joel Matthews, 2018
First Edition 1 3 5 7 9 10 8 6 4 2
ISBN: 978-1-946642-78-3
LCCN: 2018960854

Design, edits and layout: Jason Ryberg
Author photo: Joel Matthews
All rights reserved. No part of this publication may be reproduced or transmitted in any form or by any means, electronic or mechanical, including photocopying, recording or by info retrieval system, without prior written permission from the author.

Acknowledgments:

Spartan Press would like to thank Prospero's Books, The Fellowship of N-finite Jest, The Prospero Institute of Disquieted P/o/e/t/i/c/s, Will Leathem, Tom Wayne, Jeanette Powers, j. d. tulloch, Jon Bidwell, Jason Preu, Mark McClane, Tony Hayden and the whole Osage Arts Community.

This is for those who have continually supported my writing; Lori, Patricia, Ruth (my chum), Judy, Kaleen, Moe, Les, Jennifer, Alysia, Bev, and all the rest—especially Ma & Pa. This is also for all the students who have inspired me (whether they know it or not), and all the little creatures of this good earth who keep my feet on the ground and remind me of what counts.

CONTENTS

the apologetic comma / 1

where does this go? / 3

Shadow / 4

Separatists and Loyalists on the Native Prairie / 6

grace / 8

back to Nippon / 10

belly / 12

grain of rice / 14

Challenger Deep / 15

coming home / 17

while the students doodle / 20

the tiniest Japanese man I ever met / 22

Marrow / 23

Blackened toast / 25

2220 / 26

books / 27

from the inside out / 29

here / 30

The New and Improved Neanderthal / 31

the living rise / 33

the old man from Kanazawa / 34

sparrow / 36

providence / 37

sparrow number three / 39

parcel / 40

Kazakh Boy sings / 42

indomitable / 44

hero / 46

Nazarene Wren / 48

static / 51

rabbits / 52

too much / 56

an old Law / 57

working model / 59

hands / 60

lung / 62

feather / 64

tomorrow / 65

the melting of the Patagonian ice field / 67

romantic / 70

orchid origami / 71

noodle poem / 72

naked snail / 73

Common Weed / 75

Isaac, revisited / 77

*As far as we can discern, the sole purpose of
human existence is to kindle a light in
the darkness of mere being.*

-Carl Jung

This book is dedicated to Jim and Charlotte,
who have never failed to kindle a light
in the darkness.

the apologetic comma

perhaps I can imagine him as a boy
standing firm behind his mother's leg
taking it all in
a nation unto himself

and now this man
with eyes of Judo, watching
the sidewalk
blind passing feet
he goes through life confessing

sorry to step, meek feet
sorry to breathe, merciful air
never fear, brave snail
sorry to blink, favorite modest eye

he says these things in silence
tilled soil
in the rising sun

he wants to simply be a mark
not a sound, no consonant nor vowel
a space in your breath
that which draws attention to the next
not him

when he sleeps in the truck
he slumps over
chin on chest
neckbones sticking from a wooly collar
completely at ease

where does this go?

how do real poets do it?
what to put where
names, idioms,
and diction
punctuate it make it beautiful
they talk about the moon
without ever mentioning the moon
or even look up from the salamanders
to notice the once-in-a-lifetime-
occurrence:
a single drifting feather
the inner down of a Canadian goose
that chap who passed long ago overhead
calling, chatting,
punctuating

Shadow

Sitting on your lawn, your lovely lawn
Though I'm no stalker—

This Styrofoam soul does not degrade
> the memory of your touch
> your smile,
> your wriggling fishes
> and when you touched my cheek,
> I've not washed your sacred skin from mine.

If every blade of grass was a love poem
I am the plains, the tundra, the prairie, the expanse.

> Ancient fish swim in the blind muddy waters
> on a first-name basis with the terrible lizards
> they long to be frogs and toads and newts
> if only to die in the blades of love.

I breathe pollen and dust and exhaust from
metal horses
to only glimpse
> your shadow in the window
> a premonition of your form
> your lop-sided grin
> your delicate hands
> and your lazy graceful pigeon walk.

I long to count the tempo of your laughter,
the troughs of your spine
tomorrow we will be civil
pretending and abiding by norms
I pass you on my way pretending not to hear the blaring
horn of Gabriel
        pretending your subtle brow means nothing
        pretending I would not invest my life
                in your certainty
        pretending the way clothes
        hang on your frame.

And there is room in this mass of undying Styrofoam
and blades of grass
        there is room enough for smiles and walks
        and counting
        where even your fourth toe
        is reckoned worthy.
Driving is the only motion that compares
with the world zipping by unnoticed in reverie that I GO
    somewhere, anywhere
        close to your shadow, dark and blind to itself
        crawling into the light, shedding gills for lungs
        to fill this cavity.

Separatists and Loyalists on the Native Prairie

Pete Seeger once said: *Lawyers change old laws to fit new citizens.*
The nicks and cuts on my hands are a bloody witness
as I engage the fence
> new posts, stronger posts, taller posts
> new-fangled barbed wire
> and fencing pliers with scriptural eloquence.

The old fence line was for cattle, mainly Angus
it was rusty and wobbly in spots
and orioles snatched long hairs from the barbs-
> a strange harvest from a ubiquitous line.

To put herds in little boxes seemed the right thing.

It's not always greener on the other side
separatists and loyalists jeer
> through the electrified galvanized razor-

wired monstrosity
singing the same music as the democrats and
republicans
> the imperialists and the isolationists
> the red-necks and the hippies
> the Sunni and the Shia
> us and them
> me and you.

All on the same ground with only a line between,
        a line fashioned by our own hands
        only heretics and traitors cross.
The burden of engaging the fence in combat is valliant
those who take shrapnel in their flesh
those drug through the streets
those who sit at the front of the bus.
I really don't mind the nicks and cuts on my hands
        stains gathering at my feet
it's all the same stained ground with only a line between.

grace

a silted river, pregnant with deltas
defining plains, hamlets and
poppy fields

and shouldering the lazy current: ponies
and on their backs: boys
more properly: reconstructed orphans
> war
> drug-trade
> poverty
> bearing enslaved witness to violations
>> and other nasty Frankensteins
>> so easily manufactured

the boys are on break from
afternoon meditation training
> where they lie in a circle
> around the tattooed maestro:
>> *this is what it means to live*
>> *this is how*

most boys would frolic
> on this break
> in this river
> on these ponies

these boys do not
> *...this is what it means...*

they tend to ponies
> some whisper to pony ears
>> of markings
>
> others feel the scars
>> from saving ponies
>
> and a few, for the first time,
>> are living

back to Nippon

I have proposed to you five times:

the first on
white sands
when I braided your locks

the second
proudly
amid glistening buildings
sky-scraping things

the third
at a park
in South America
when you laughed
at the bracelet I gave you

the fourth
in New York City
in a boat
on a river
and I gave you a necklace
and you cried

and the fifth

at home
after a bit of rice
and onion
and beef
and I bent a knee
whispered an ancient
Haiku
my ever-love
I know no other sun

belly

270 dayears
I am Jo…Jo…Jonah
years marked by meals of krill
        and deep sea giganto squid

3's, 9's, and 3's
are the mark on my head
        our heads a-fla…fla…flopping when we tire
        when we are on full-term tenterhooks

such Arabic magic
        serves only
        to point
        to the point

at one time, admiring the shells
those primordial mobile homes
        an oyster's scuttle bemused
the day I was ready I did not know
        was The Day
                and now I relish giganto squid
                      such strange happenings
                      such
                              strange happenings

what are you people doing up there?!
I'm certain 7's are part of the magic
(Greed, Gluttony, Sloth, Envy, you know the routine)
but I'll be damned if I can fig...fig...figure it out!
and I guess I am just that
> left craving fresh greens,
> the sunrise,
> and a shed husk

grain of rice

it has been said a rice
grain contains the universe

names and scriptures are written on
rice grains
prophets and prophecies on these
slivers of the moon reflecting
race and tribe
grains
feeding
old women who tell tales
of great floods, the seven thrown stones
grains
feeding
barefoot children
playing prophet in the rain

Challenger Deep

> *(*Challenger Deep is the deepest part of the deepest oceanic trench on earth, in the neighborhood of 36,201 feet below sea level.)*

We stand on the abyssal plain
where there's no brome grass, katydids, bison,
nor spring zephyrs.
Here we dispense of social convention
and the blather of niceties as
eight tons per square inch make us desperate
for even a singular bubble of air.

Do you feel that?
My toes are warm, and yours?
This tectonic plate is holy wafer thin here,
       step lightly, or
           we shall join the infernal comedy.

Let us decide by rock, paper, scissors
who will step off this last cliff next.
The winner will jump,
and the loser stay with a bundle of rope and
angel hair
       just in case
       the gulper eel hungers,

        the dragonfish awakens, or
        an intrepid Moby Dick meanders by.

One, two
and your paper covers my rock.
Best of three? I thought not.
So here I stand
again
seems I've set up shop on the abyssal plain,
cavorting with nematodes and
dazily swirling my finger in Paleolithic silt,
lost in ancient spirals
        with angel hair.

coming home

i think my mittens are
frozen

driving cold
snow
beating down
keeping our people
inside
huddled
around pots of beans
and borscht

with heavy
coat
woolly hat
mother says not
to wander far
i am her little boy
father tells of
a brother lost to the blinding white gale
i am his little boy
and my little sister looks
with heavy lost eyes

i think my mittens are
frozen

my toes no longer answer
yet

among laden spruce
a single dove has flown

i think my mittens are
frozen
my toes no longer answer
and yet
here

i hear
eyes closed
among childless falling flakes
voices of angels
coming down
doves flying home

my mittens are frozen
yet here
they curl back and
ring like bells
pealing bells

i hear ferocity
unfettered frenzy and zeal
voices so raw

i feel my toes again
voices so strong
this little boy finds his way back
to our humble shack
kiss mother and father
put my worried sister to bed
tell her a new story

while the students doodle

i am certain i take my words seriously
because i am a teacher
and while i teach
the students doodle

doodle spiderwebs
are they to catch thoughts and ideas
or simply life as it is?
the life of a student is
complicated
demanding
it is difficult to be young
joyful, vibrant, but ripe
with challenge

doodle warriors
clad in armor and wielding swords
i will award you extra credit
to wrestle
that hero
no mercy, no tap-outs
be clad and wield, youngling

doodle boxes and shapes
sketch the marathon to perfect form
to a so-very-distant horizon

cubes
cylinders and
tetrahedrons
that which contains
which defines
the shape of the future
of you

doodle faces, faces with tears
i know those big questions
but do not know
the big answers
here i doodle for you
a side-road with deep ruts
and now
a footpath
softly trodden
with high grass and wildflowers
to either side
something worth exploring
which i take very seriously

the tiniest Japanese man I've ever met

double-majored
took thirty credit hours one semester
and was so full of manners you'd think the guy would
explode from pathological propriety

the tiniest Japanese man I've ever met
saw a string of green holiday lights in a window
trying to be a tree
and said it was Godzilla

he shared soup
savory crackers
and squid jerky
he was on time
on his game

I confess there are times
I'd like to pull him out of my pocket
if only to hear him cuss in
my language after a long week
    when he felt betrayed
or have him ask where the monkey are in Kansas
    as we drive down the road
and then enjoy a good chat

I suppose
I can now see
obliviously it was Godzilla

Marrow

Forty days in the shower
to wash away grey obsessions
        condition my mind to freedom
        and exfoliate Svengali.

The shopping list is:
dog food, eggs, rice, and frozen pizza…
because I am a lazy man
because I want it now here as I please, please
and the damnable aisle seven,
the ramen noodles I love.

I think I know the mind of the war-time presidents
regretful indulgences and obligations
but I've no bomb to drop…
        save the delicate autistic world I've created.

All the while you walk by blind
sucking the marrow from my spine.

Days in the shower are not doing it for me,
not the way your smile does
or the way you blink your eyes.

Call me jangle-bones then,
I am the music of coins in my empty pocket
> a-rattling
> a-rattling
So call me jangle-bones, empty bones
who needs marrow anyway?
> All it does is make blood.
I will fill my veins with coffee, with ale, with
prescribed elixirs from Germanic ancients
> my body will thrive on secret imaginings,
> and with that

I'll keep my one-trick-pony mind
I'll keep showering and rattling
and jangling
jangling.

Blackened Toast

A world of order
ticking to the time promised by
Swiss watchmakers.

It's a long fall from heaven's throne.

Home late from work
        chaos stepping in to make all lights red and
        dizzy children darting to the yellow lines
the mathematician calculates the hour precisely
and scowls at the cat lazily greeting him,
        knowing she never colored inside the lines.

Home late from work
a tiny gnat in the ointment
is an aneurism in the regimented order
and begins as a spring thaw trickle of leaving
the porch light on
and ends in a cascade of confusion with
        missed programs on the tele
        neglecting
the morning's anti-fungal foot-cream ritual
        and never stopping to think what's beneath
            the black ruination of toast.

2220

*Guest number twenty-two
twenty, your order is ready.*

It is a corned beef sandwich,
nothing flashy
something to match my shoes and my
mood. Today is a day I need
to fly under the radar
a stealthy ghost.

He calls out order after
order, that deep smoky voice, a colossal bell tolling
is that the sound cranes hear before
they dance? Or
is it the last sound I'll ever want to hear?
A perfect ending to a clever
iconoclastic play, the type of ending that-
-like a shoe and a sandwich-
flies under the ultra sound, the type of ending
only subterranean critters fathom.

Every call becomes a new plot
a new dance, another heirloom pocket-watch
with engravings like:
 …with love, or
 …always yours, or
 …this is my heart keeping your life orderly.

books

What matters more:
a history,
or the author?

Old women who refuse to die,
flowers on the grave—
not the stone—
build histories.
Refugee children who live hard stories
tough survivors—
not victors—
build histories.

Is it so much a tree fell on my house,
or that it was my house?
Perhaps I should be
asking
old women
and refugee
children.

>Dirt and catfish
>know these things,
>they smell of

both history
and author.
Digging and noodling,
tilling and scavenging
the whiskers sense a past—
        and send the catfish
        writing in the mud
        hoping against hope
        someone reads it.

from the inside out

how utterly terrifying it would have been
to be
in that mob
see Samson pick
up that
jawbone and
begin to kill
hip and thigh

oh promised one!

isn't that from an ass?

and in the end
running mad

Lordy
in the end
how we all are him

here

the Yeti likes it here
up north too many
too many Yeti
up north

without his hair
the Yeti seems as
me
clipped and trimmed
cleaned, gleaming and
passing

The New and Improved Neanderthal

Us, we modern ones
hunt for the closest parking spots
and fill our carts with name brand, not generic goods.
We pay the dues of hides, shiny stones,
and pretty feathers
with the deft wave of a Master Card key fob
encoded with DNA imprint sequences
and retinal scans.

We cerebral Cro Magnons
litter the veld with constructed caves
with central cooling machinery
and a stocked wine cooler
(each bottle captured live in the wilds).
Cave paintings now called abstract art
represent a most distorted story of the hunt
and visions of the shaman.

The spear of point and click
is effortless hunting, sitting-down hunting.
Easily caught is the prey of a neoprene chin-strap
to stop me from snoring,
a new mate,
enrollment in a subversive parochial movement,
and epic stories of time-bending neutrinos, winking
electrons, and the space between.

All easily caught, passive prey.

Some of us used to excel with gazelles,
but now hunt the popular vote
or the revered greenback.

Us sly sapiens
hunt the most bizarre of beasts
gather the most bizarre goods
and gazelles are still
gazelles.

the living rise

when humans gather together
all together
swaying in time
my arm on your shoulder
and yours on mine
speaking in cherub

the holy man
from Istanbul
says:
ashes to ashes and dust to dust
the time between is our fire

the living rise
as long-legged storks
wading,
catching minnows
the living are
playing the lyre and singing
heavenly operas of falling leaves and
the snow on cats
who wander winter streets

the old man from Kanazawa

sits in a park
under blooming trees
beside a stepping
castle stream

he once mined gold
now a simple farmer
of potatoes
the shamisen in gnarled hands
ancient as the memory
of grass
plays
simply

his time is near
he knows: why else would his jacket
lay on the cold stone beside him?
he breaks for
a sip of tea
hint of breeze
in his short hair

and thinks of potatoes
fed to now
sleeping children,
innocent sprouts for tomorrow

so as not to be lost in translation:
his name
written properly
means:
small warrior beside dragon
which
now that he sees the waters again
is to be
his last song
last potato
for him
only

he sings of a sparrow
brown
common
simple
and elegant
all at once
flying over mountains
spending its last breath
for the Emperor
who heard
that day only one song
from the trees
in bloom

sparrow

ten, twelve, twenty...
times he heard the voice
and sparrow learned to speak crane

the master expected
sparrow to light in his palm again,
but alas, never again
will he feel his beloved this way

yet the freed sparrow returns,
but long enough to sing in crane
and fly away
carrying light with
leaving light behind

when joy rises in the morn
cold goes to sleep
and the old master wakes
to the song of a new crane

providence (sparrow, revisited)

There's a Special Providence in the Fall of a Sparrow.
-Hamlet Act 5, scene 2

little one of hollow bone
feather
a drop of blood
and endless chatter
how i mourn your fall
who will care for
your babies?
who will bring them
to flight
and the beauty of sparrow?

i am not so much a believer in many things
but i believe in life
so here i will stop
build your pyre
befriend silence for your providence

inside it seems empty now
and i question ruthlessly:
why you, innocent one?
where is the King of Birds today,
your shepherd?

some days i light a candle
i do not know why
perhaps it is the flame, flickering
with a type of life
perhaps it is the dripping wax
a memory
building upon itself
perhaps it is you
and what i still hear

sparrow number three

we cleaned these floors
or
clean enough i can eat here
i know i'm made of star-stuff
overhead the last sparrow flies
we saw her fly
we held a holy service for her
(i carry something in my pocket)
did we hear the walls come down?
are we truly us now?
have the arguments stopped, the bombs held?
i hope this is no dream
i've had so many
watching children save dolphins
watching men save children
watching women save men
watching trees put out the fire
the watcher being watched
the third sparrow in my pocket
she wakes

parcel

Buddha came through the mail today
in a flimsy box
the postmaster had no celebration for the event
      no sand paintings in the language of
      symbolism
      no prayer flags fluttering
      no bringing together of the hands nor bowing
      not even a simple Namaste
      just a flimsy box
      a plain flimsy box
            no fancy labels
            no foreign tongue
            no warnings of fragility and no gaudy
            stamps of insurance values
            and conditions thereof

a plain flimsy box
that was, as it seems it should be,
a bit lop-sided
one side heavy:
      to remind me of the dead wood in my life
one side light:
      to remind me of how things can be
and just as it should be:
      to remind me of the perfection

I suspect some prophets
travel only in First Class
> their posh private jets
> instant feed satellite connections
> rare exquisite wines
> priceless trappings galore
> and an entourage of sycophants groveling
> something about not being worthy

Buddha came
from that plain flimsy box
a bit dusty,
just like the rest of us in this real life
as it should be

Kazakh Boy Sings
(an amateur video)

on this internet,
this steampunk series of tubes and trucks
I watch this boy sing
a ridiculously hopeful ditty
his cross-cut home-do hair-do, his jet cap
and ancestral garb of sandstone russet with
nugget-gold piping
maybe he's six
or seven
holding nothing back
little feet stepping
he's doing it well
doing it right
old fathers nod
old mothers smile
it is the day of Victory
over fascism
who better to sing this song?

and I don't know a single word
(except the hope underneath)
just as I don't know
how many shoulders he stands on
and if the hope is any sign

knowing the words doesn't matter
the same as when his mother first sung this to him
this jingle,
this catchy little ditty
she sang when he was blue
after a nightmare
or perhaps
when he woke early the first morning to ride his
new proud pony

and I do not know a word
and my bones sing along
that deepening rattling of
old fathers keeping the faith despite the occupation
old mothers nursing a rich future on a proud past
and old ponies
old faithful companions who sometimes make
the best of humans
galloping to this song
hooves clapping Victory over fascism
hooves crossing the steppes
cresting the sun

indomitable

If this silly sun
would only stop shining for once
I could be depressed again,
maybe write something
about Death
Or loosing the soles from my shoes of hope.

To not force a smile
is a good.
Even if this paralyzed grin
deepens the crow's feet grips,
it is still a good
and reminds me of mother's cooking—

home-made egg noodles
Do you want skinny ones or fat ones?
And rhubarb cobbler that wrote epic
tales by itself
where the fuzzy things win, the green things survive
and the cold icicles of fear are transformed
returned and recycled
into life-blood.

It is that time in the semester
where there's no time

only grading reading grading reading grading
and shambling,
…my clackety skellington vibrating
with neutrinos and bird song and the negative white
space on paper.
Shambling
into class—just a little late,
as if teaching were an afterthought.

There is no time right now
and my watch, my daily planet tracker, knows this
on occasion it stops of it's own accord
reminding me to breathe.
Stopping to remind me yet again

that's all there is, is time
and shoes that never give out.

hero

stick-figure boy
a student, delicate sparse Chinese character
    with a rare mark to the side

early June morning
he had had enough
of enough
and drew a line
on the tarmac
—

nurses cried last night
women hauled in on park benches
three students on the back of a rickshaw driver who
rested a bullet in his own liver
last night
nurses cried
—

but on this June morning,
enough was enough
before a legion of machines
one figure
armed
with
a bag

did he wave his homework in front of a line of tanks
to stop them all?
was it his lunch? noodles, a bit of chicken,
and some greens?
dare I ask if it was a bag of letters from his
grandmother
who had survived three wars,
two cultural revolutions,
and a life of hard work,
       who said she could never
              be more proud?

stick-figure student
bag in hand
stopping tanks
what is your rare beautiful mark?

Nazarene Wren
(Corinthians 11:24 – Of the Jews
five times received I forty stripes save one.)

Forty stripes, save one
Is the sun setting or rising? Coming or going?
I've lost track
The flesh is thick
        As pregnant air under green skies.
Under herringbone weave
        Pale frame, bright in the sun, agrees
        From belief, from the gut
And the timbers are heavy
        With memory
        With intent
        With desire
        With allowance

Forty stripes save one
Am I coming or going? Setting or rising?
It all seems the same, tastes the same
        Like all winter days
        And the Shellyesque violets screaming:
It is spring! It is spring!
And the timbers say the same
        Wooden homes
        Wooden careers
        Wooden lives
        Wooden loves.

Forty stripes save one
Are those stripes mine?
I've had so many
  usually none are saved
It has become
  the Rosetta Stone…this herringbone flesh

A wren's delicate footprints in a dust of snow
  Divine punctuation
  Numinous white contrast
Slow and deliberate, on hands and knees
  Prostrate
  I follow her tracks
  Gently and romantically
  Never disturbing the dusting
  Revering the stark frozen water that cannot
  yet be drunk unto the earth
  Lost in her hieroglyphs
  I forget the stripes
  The day, the motion, the number
    For they are so beautiful
    So delicious to my eyes

  The design of something greater whispers…
    I crane my neck to hear…
      Just one syllable…
      A single utterance…

A tiny drift in the snow-dust
    A ripple of white
    How odd…

        Oh, the inconstance
        Damn you life
        Damn your infidelity
        Give me her stripes,
          I will invent mercy
            I will be her Simon.

Her feathers, perfect creations,
    Shone through
    A flash of brown in the mass of white
        No tears do her justice.
        All grief infantile.

And I saw them.
The last hieroglyphs she wrote.
    Her last mortal markings.
Yes, I saw them.
And in reading them,
    In knowing them,
All stripes are saved.

static

having been told I was:
called out
my first thought was:
to where?

I stand right here
everyone knows
salt, wind, blood, and mud
it matters not
for here I am,
like usual
again.

I should say something?
what more can I say
than this?
(like usual)

it's not like I stand under mountains
      or to the side of the plains

these are the plains on top of the mountains
in case you didn't notice
is this view not magnificent?

rabbits

summer, 1936, Gage County Kansas
the dustbowl been around for a few years
and I's only 14 in '36
in '35 the grasshoppers ate everythin
even pitchfork handles left out
it was the most damnedable tough times I ever did see
so '36 looked good for us on the farm
until the jack-rabbits came
outta nowheres
they's all over, everywhere
we had acres of alfalfa for the cattle
ate up overnight
and I ain't never seen Pa so damn mad
so he got up with some neighbor men
herded them rabbits up in a pen
hundreds
thousands of 'em
all hoppin and a-jumpin
and I's thinkin I'd be eatin rabbit for weeks…

then Pa and the men got out clubs
you ever heard a rabbit death-cry?
ever heard it again and again
and again
hundreds of times?

and again
that cryin they make, that screamin
hidin in the barn didn't help
it's worse than little children with the fever
even worse than Ma with that still-born little sister
I coulda had
I ain't never ate rabbit since

in '41 I's shipped off to Europe under Old Glory
I went off to set a-right all that wrong
and killed my first man…
he screamed like one of them damn rabbits
screamed and screamed so I shot him again
I still see his eyes at night
I remember waking up one night in a trench thinking
I was dreaming about Pa swingin that club
but it was only Jenkins, that tall boy from Cincinnati
wondering where the hell his leg was
now, you understand here I ain't never held a man
like that before,
but I was there to right what was wrong
and Jenkins was a good man
but I couldn't take his screamin no more
I needed them dreams to stop

in '50 I was called back by Uncle Sam
and sent to Korea
and oh, Lordy, things was different

I had little babies lookin to me
and I's just a kid myself
but I had a job to do
we set ourselves up a trap one day
and Lewis, damn I liked that boy,
he…I think he was from Virginia
(we used to make fun of his accent)
anyways, he gave up his life
drawing them into our trap
so we shot 'em all down to a man—
each one screamin, that's all I heard
all I seen was them eyes of that Kraut boy I kilt,
my Pa raisin that club high in the air
ready to come down
in '52 I got my dumb-ass self booby-trapped
saw my leg paint the underbrush all up in red
I spent two days and nights screamin on and off
like that Jenkins boy
wonderin where the hell my leg was

and now,
here I finally been able to sleep again
and it's '07
a time I ain't never thought I'd be seein
I got kids, grandkids, and greatkids
but here I am at 85 beatin the odds
I've worn out three fake legs already
and I wake up in the VA

at Joshua's bedside
holdin his hand,
wantin to hold him like that Jenkins boy
he's my greatkid back from Iraq
and he wakes up screaming
wonderin where the hell his damn leg is
all I hear
for 71 years
is them rabbits

too much

too much of a good thing can
burn
and
bless

today it seems i can bend boards
as if i can stretch the keel of life
manta rays see it coming
and while flying away
call their friends, saying:
this is unheard of

it seems as if there can be too much trust
but that is a lie
there can never be too much trust
never too much green
never too many leaves on a tree
nor too many soft words spoken

an old goat stares at the moon
wondering
until the kids run up
stumbling jumping and running
the kids run up

an old Law

it was said by the ancients:
one should ask one's guardian angels to
stay
when one engages the unclean

guardian angel?
do I truly need guarding?
have I mistaken this reckless abundance?
when I see a girl save
a worm from the sidewalk,
did I not just witness a guardian angel?
how about: Spirits Who Have Joined Up?

I find myself regretful
for keeping these angels near when I lied
or cheated
or bore false witness against myself
how much shame for me did I subject Them to?
are They still here? did I flirt with The
Book of the Forsaken?
what tar lay on Their downy skin
because of me?
and who have I
been to do that?

a pendulum must swing twice for
every second: up and back again
and now that I'm swinging back again
        judging by the creeping Promethean grey
in my beard
I have eyes that might see
                what is wild and what
                is not
                the contrast of love
                and fear
                and every choice between

now I ask Those Who Have Joined Up
to delight
in the saving of a worm

working model

i want to be separate from
you
to know cat from dog
where this working model goes and if
it was a good idea at the time
i want to miss you more
than wanting to be there

hands

84 years old and he was
humble as a naked snail.
He was along for the ride
with his daughter in law
who spoke about inter-faith relations.

84 years short and sturdy
a fireplug
every follicle seemingly intact
bright and gentle eyes
coated with the dust of age.

84 years and saying *nice to have met you*
and *it has been a pleasure*
his hand clasped in mine,
the stout clamp
only 84 years can rally.

before we closed I
discovered
he had been an internal surgeon for fifty-odd years
and his hand was in mine

watches and clocks and sundials and hourglasses and
every satellite
stopped
the entire universe froze.

wounded organs, praying families,
delicate sutures and bold incisions
flashed in my mind
fifty-odd years of healing
and his most trusted tool in my sophomoric hand
dumbly, all I do
is to utter *These hands…*
and his grin
started the universe again.

lung

precious children forget your name
        don't know Stone
        let alone Tide and Ferns
someone else walks with the generations
you have sired

Shinto in an iron lung
I will fold my wings to be near you

I will stop breathing to sing with you
we can learn Sufi together, you and I

I will not father to hear of ancestry
only you can draw those lines

since I've folded my wings thrice-over
will you join me in living Nature?

I will poem rural Illinois
after nightly rains, under the June moon
hearing Corn grow

will you poem elder Rabbits
and sly Deer creeping from pines
to nibble Cabbage?

I have no choice but to be honest
here holding my breath
childless, folded wings and all
it is my intent to replace you in this iron lung
I can live in the machine
better you walk

feather

we sing of careless love—
falling with no thought of self
we sing of cool water—
sweet mercy of earth

and in between we walk as if
we see the nature of things

once
on the shoulders of friends
i reached high at a vision
and caught
a silken angel feather

here
look

tomorrow,
or
the day

i take my leave from you, here
is a big river
flowing out to something
more than both of us
as many things are
but
i will say as big as your best horse running
across steppe and field
rose, dandelion
and weepy delphinium watching

river
here is a big
river for you, flowing
with little minnows
who know every stone
who jump for the sun
jump for you

in the name of our ancestors
we who have stood
on the shoulders of giants
i promise

when i am the minnow
tomorrow
i will jump higher than any other
and give you a wink
you will know it is me
jumping for your sun

the melting of the Patagonian ice field

I.
sleeping frozen water
what is it you dream?
flight? teeth? becoming gin?

little rabbits
great flightless birds
perhaps a bit bigger than we had hoped
and guanacos have agreed
it is time to watch the ice

II.
out of sight, out of mind
and spider sticks his head in the sidewalk crack
I know full well he sees me seeing him
both wondering
of my shoes
and spider stays when
I stop to wonder if anyone is watching
that is
other than spider and I

III.
when the pooling begins
and dreaming stops

it's still soft, downy
the sound of sun from here beside daisies, rabbits

svelte guanacos leap across the water
stones and moss become a blur
they go to whisper
to tapirs
listen for the ice

IV.
no one is watching
so we share a moment
spider and I
eyeing
but just a moment, after all
my shoes still count, and
he is still sticking his head in the sidewalk crack
seeing me seeing him

V.
waking water runs dancing
the break-fast luscious
the look on faces of meditating catfish
is enough in itself
the Patagonian ice field
has given way

the greening and the following of things
flora and fauna tango
birds and little berries
rabbits and endless green
and the guanaco babies prancing about,
as if they were first firsts

VI.
walking away
no one sees me looking back
I wonder of all the years ever spent by anyone
in Tibet
years resting between spider and I
how many did we see?
my shoes still counting
his head in the sidewalk crack
seeing me seeing him

Romantic

the romantic ones
pine away
wanting to be your heart
the seat of love

boring
being a heart is boring
it does one thing:
beat
it stays in one place
and never touches you
might as well be
liver
or spleen

i want to be your first
metacarpal
the first bone
of your lovely thumb
make you opposable
give you dexterity,
allow you to grasp
a brush
a pencil
a key
or work a pair of lacquered
chopsticks with mother of pearl inlay

orchid origami

white rice paper folding into
itself and out to
this big fat weepy universe

orchids
white orchids fold the thin paper of
ancestors, both wise and foolish
fold into the shape of memory

mother brewing soup
father cleaving wood
brother laughing
sister with a kitten
that small life knows only trust

we will forge this world into life
a kitten
trusts the look
in our eye
the white paper orchid
most simple thing
the best fold

noodle poem

seven noodles fill my bowl

one for the king, for what is due
one for the queen, none more fair
one to lay at the temple doorstep
one for my child, for a happy belly
one for the chicken, for tomorrow's egg
one for me—I like noodles
and one final noodle
to tie high in the shushing pine
for the glamour of wind

naked snail

...and I prayed to have some response to the things that were so clearly beautiful to me...

-Leonard Cohen

in the midst of all things
my economy, desires, and daily workings
I notice the naked snail
that slimy stretch of flesh
bravely crossing the sidewalk
in a frame of time different than mine
it is their pilgrimage
of a year
belly-down and
ravenous

clearly beautiful to me

to what temple do they tread?
where is their Angkor Wat?
I've not seen it, or rather, do not recall
ever having seen a cathedral of clover
a wild mustard mosque
a brome grass basilica
nor any Stonehenge of dandelions
for what temple do they risk a year of their lives?

clearly beautiful to me

I don't pray for a response
perhaps I'm lucky
to respond reflexively
perhaps my first and second brains are interchanged
with cortex in my belly
and gut in my skull
I respond reflexively

I've never seen a naked turtle
nor a naked lobster
but I've seen the naked snails on their pilgrimage
bravely facing simian feet
and hot sun
on their sacred sojourn to
higher places
to respond

Common Weed

at the slagheap
the corner of ironworks and diesel garage
lie cesspools of spoiled oil

the morning shelter of behemoths
brutes infected with the blight of disuse who refuse
to decay under scabs of rust because
        memories of the war to end all wars
        have been so rudely forgotten
        in favor of lip-syncing bleached poppies
the half-track hot box
lends the slightest advantage, just enough
for roots to find purchase
and feeble leaves unraveling
        to sing praise of radiation
        and photosynthetic brilliance

daily workers drag their bodies from warm beds
carry their fuel in brown bags and superhero tins
pass by the Common Weed
utter sentences of doom
cast scorn at the noxious one

I am John Q. Common Weed
growing here above the septic tank

watching the cesspool portents
and admiring the sculptures of rubbish
I am sick with life,
> the intrepid wonder of my limits
> my roots spiraling through the black carbon
> forging their way to my Missing Piece

Isaac, Revisited

it was here upon this stone I grew
old ninety years ago
threadbare
prone
my father looming above
the sun
counting time
blinding my skin and the
living things

I remember as a child
jumping into every clay pot
knowing I would
find
water
the maker
stars
a smiling woman in the street
discipline of
a working man
a sleeping shepherd

father did not approve
Abraham was a busy man
for a wet boy

there were
keys and footsteps
father's old metal authority
and how I knew
how he walked up these steps
it was not
hesitation
but
the surety of the passing sun

it was under that sun I lay back
then
all I could see
father towering trembling
above
a wren in his chest
score of
demons about him
he's praying
to be as steady as my mother
if just one key fit
that one closed door
if enough praise
will keep the sun near

I remember as a child…
…I…
remember

as a child
the hushing of people
when I drew near
whispers of my father
one hundred
a dawn
whispers of the voice of
water
and me not
able to say

I remember as a child
running from poets
minstrels
bringing me too close
to night
and the sun
at once together

father did not approve
aBrahman is one
after all
he held a key up on high
talking
uncertain about the certainty
of that key
if there is only one

he missed this stone
a thing
of many the sun
sees

there was
at a point a
thing
under this sun
a tear of Enoch
father took for God
and I walked away
with blind
old Samson
like blind old me
standing here
did I tell you it was this
very stone?

Joel E Matthews is a Nebraska-born farm-boy who left the corn fields for the wheat fields of Kansas. His first life was as a psychotherapist, where he learned how to put ego aside and walk for miles in shoes not his own. His second, and current, life is as a univer sity instructor where he gets paid to be a nerd about science, culture, and other cool things. You can frequently find him standing outside talking to birds, bugs, squirrels, and the many rabbits who live in his unkempt backyard. He can also be found in his other natural habitat: the couch; where he reads, writes, watches documentaries, and plays with Lego bricks.

This project was made possible, in part, by generous support from the Osage Arts Community.

Osage Arts Community provides temporary time, space and support for the creation of new artistic works in a retreat format, serving creative people of all kinds — visual artists, composers, poets, fiction and nonfiction writers. Located on a 152-acre farm in an isolated rural mountainside setting in Central Missouri and bordered by ¾ of a mile of the Gasconade River, OAC provides residencies to those working alone, as well as welcoming collaborative teams, offering living space and workspace in a country environment to emerging and mid-career artists. For more information, visit us at www.osageac.org

www.ingramcontent.com/pod-product-compliance
Lightning Source LLC
Chambersburg PA
CBHW020127130526
44591CB00032B/553